Words from the Well of Wisdom

Aphorisms

by
Laurie Farnell

GW00670920

© Laurie Farnell 2017

Published by Converge at York St John University
              Lord Mayor's Walk
              York
              YO31 7EX

converge@yorksj.ac.uk

All rights reserved. This book or any portion thereof may not be reproduced or used in any manner without the express written permission of the publisher, except for the use of brief quotations in a book review.

The rights of Laurie Farnell to be identified as the author of this work have been asserted in accordance with the Copyright, Designs and Patents Act 1988.

A CIP catalogue record for this book is available from the British Library.

ISBN 978-1-9999002-0-5

Typesetting – Mark Heslington

Contents

CONTENTS

Introduction

Welcome to my first published book. A book I had no intention of putting together until prompted by others.

I began to write these aphorisms as a way of coping with severe depression which I have suffered from since childhood. I discovered quite by accident that when I was going 'into' an episode, my mind could slip into a crevasse of the deepest thought. It felt like a bleak and bottomless well but, luckily, an occasional ripple of light from below would reveal itself and so I began to write these aphorisms.

For a considerable period of my life I became homeless and as a way of keeping body and soul together it became a habit to write down my thoughts. It gave me a wonderful way to express myself as I had very few friends at that time. My great love was walking, and this is when I began to think and write, always carrying a small writing book as I went along. I taught myself to draw, then wrote over my drawings to save paper.

I had little money and would sleep in old barns, empty garages, anywhere I could find. Sometimes graveyards, where I knew no one would bother me except the dead. Once I enjoyed the perfect convenience of a telephone box. One day when sleeping rough, I lost my writing book. It was then that I realised how important this book was to me. There was no doubt it had become my faithful guide and companion.

Although I knew I suffered from depression, I didn't realise it was an illness I could get help with and it was my writing that helped keep body and soul together. One day, things got so bad that in rags I literally crawled on my hands and knees into a doctor's surgery. So finally, ending years of timeless wandering, my illness was diagnosed and treated, and I spent a few months in hospital. When I came out I was offered adequate housing. But then came the long and difficult task of readjustment for I found living in a house no easy matter. To me it felt like a prison. I missed the wide open sky and the closeness to nature that had so sustained me.

Again though, creativity came to my aid and now having bought a guitar, I began to write songs. My long development as a poet helped me to write lyrics. Around this time, a friend introduced me to Converge at York St John's University. He was doing drama and thought this might help me. How can I ever explain the difference it's made? Since joining Converge I have never looked back. I've made new friends, begun to develop my writing, learnt new skills and sing in a choir. For once, I feel I belong somewhere. I've become part of a community where I'm not labelled or judged. It has been a real inspiration and joy to work with others who have struggled like me and see them truly blossom.

I hope you find this book of aphorisms thought provoking, amusing and relevant to your life; that they speak to you and inspire you, whatever your circumstances.

Laurie Farnell
20th September 2017

10/13/06

It seems a strange thing that light comes out of darkness, strength from gentleness.

Time

Good advice is only good when it comes at the right moment.

To be born in a certain time is like a prison we cannot escape from. Confined to the limits of our knowledge, the technology of the day, only our imagination, like a free bird, can pass between the bars of our confinement.

When the mind is fully engaged
and locked in gear, time
mysteriously disappears.

A camera captures a moment
in time, but an artist can live
in a timeless moment.

For those looking for time,
children play there.

Time is never a true gauge of
how old you think you are.

Animosity, like an old thorn,
sharpens with time.

It's always tempting to see the world through rose-tinted glasses, but in reality they were poorly made and rather expensive.

Talent without industry is lost to time.

Time must be relative to size; a fly sees us in slow motion but for its speed we cannot catch it, yet we share the same space and time.

Our lives are like a mayfly; a few wing beats in time, counting the dawn and dusk of our existence.

Time uncovers all mysteries; all knowledge, all truths emerge in the daylight of reason.

Time has made the spider wise, but not the fly.

Going back to the past is like going back to bed after getting up; nothing ever comes of it.

What counts in life is not time,
but the absence of time.

To focus on one thing at a time
is to lose all sense of it, to be the
master, not the slave of it.

Time you enjoy bears the fruit
of time; time for others is to
sow a seed in time.

You cannot go backwards in
time, experience is forged in time.

Now is always the right time
for immediate action.

– TIME –

To daydream is to enter the
world before time began.

Time is a spiral staircase
that all life treads upon.

Time unlocks all mysteries
if we go back far enough
to find the key.

There is a dawn and
dusk to all things.

Our body has a clock, but
thought has no sense of time.

Enquiry is the root of
all knowledge; time the
fruit of all wisdom.

Getting older is like arriving
in the future, but with the
wrong suitcases.

Life

To progress is to remember
what we've learnt from the
mistakes that we've forgotten.

All adventures start
with a dream imagined.

An adventure is only an
adventure when things go wrong.

Every pack of cards needs a
jester, so it is in life.

To walk in wisdom is to know
the measure of many things.

Prepare your food with the
reverence that befits a life.

I always find the stories in the
newspaper fascinating just before
I light the fire with them.

Beware those who make a
virtue out of ignorance.

Aphorisms and mathematics
have a common cause.

There is a saboteur within us,
just waiting for us to be
complacent and thoughtless; it
loves to catch us unawares.

One should respect traditions,
but with an open and
questioning mind.

When clearing out the
cupboard, sweep your fears
out with the cobwebs.

When I see a little bug on my
book, I don't kill it, for one day
we could be swopping places, I
believe that all life has
consciousness at some level.

People fly off to find
paradise, when it's waiting
on their doorstep.

You cannot argue against logic
without good reason.

Experience is a rock we can step
up to and speak from.

There are those who
talk too much and their
ears stop working.

Alcohol feeds our mood
but dampens our spirits.

To appreciate and savour life,
to wonder at it! Surely these
are our greatest riches.

At the appropriate level, anger
can be a motivating force for
change, pushing through
difficulties, a form of
empowerment.

Beware when we swear,
for we curse ourselves.

Wisdom is like looking down the
wrong end of a telescope, but
seeing the bigger picture.

To show compassion for
life is to value your own.

To climb a mountain takes
motivation, challenge and risk;
life is a mountain.

A break away can give a fresh
look, a new perspective on life.

Sometimes it's not what
people say, it's what they don't
say that is so revealing.

There is no blessing like children
to fix our lives, root us in the
earth and a common mind, bind
souls together for all eternity.

Bullies seek power; victims
give theirs away.

Failure can break you,
or make you stronger.

Like water, intelligence
seeks its own level.

Count your close friends as
your fortune, not money.

Possessions are a burden we must
always carry; enlightenment
means exactly what it says.

To jest is to make a mockery
of the truth, and a feast
of our fears.

We become what we think
we are; thoughts can free
you or enslave you.

Envy is an unwelcome
compliment from the
incompetent.

You cannot advise
one who isn't seeking.

To befriend others is a fine
thing, a blessing often
returned, unbeknown.

In company spare your words
and listen well, then you can
think before you speak.

What is excellence
but a discerning eye
and an attentive ear?

The secret of alcohol
moderation is to drink beer like
wine, drink wine like a liqueur,
and treat spirits as a very rare and
occasional phenomenon.

Split hairs on a deal with the
shopkeeper, not your friends.

A compliment from the heart is
worth a roomful of speeches.

There is great comfort
in distraction.

The secret of poetry is to seek
the end before the beginning.

The best antidote to worry is
action of any kind.

We marvel at birds at how they
fly; their freedom, effortless poise
and grace; a bicycle, to me, has
much the same qualities.

To be really sorry is to
admit our weaknesses.

Intuition begins as a feeling, then
slowly turns to certainty.

In trying to please others, we
sometimes make a rod for our
own backs; such is the hold of
our insecurities.

To run a marathon one must
first set a distance you can
easily manage.

People don't remember,
but what was done to them,
they do to you.

Heed your instincts;
doubt is a canny fellow.

To find a truth, we must shift a
mountain of ignorance, a shovel
full of half-truths, and a sieve
full of speculation.

You cannot jump up ten flights
of stairs in one go; solve
problems one step at a time.

Make a good start if you
mean to finish well.

Drugs pollute the mind, insult
the body and scatter the soul.

No amount of food and drink
can satisfy an empty life.

Better to take action, than pray
for the welfare of others.

Open your mind then
your eyes will be opened.

Prejudice has deep roots in the unkempt garden of ignorance.

There is something Gestapo-like about the high heel; the look and sound is all about power.

When men smoke large fat cigars they are alluding to something small about themselves.

A person can be a closed book, but a laugh reveals all.

Self-esteem is often a gift from others.

Approach learning as if
you know nothing but
question everything.

To change your life,
change your habits.

When we get stuck it's for a
reason. Have a break, go for a
walk, visit a friend.

In life, learning needs a counter-
balance to move forward.

Life is a journey, a road
interweaving through the
lives of others, weaving a
coat of many colours.

Take heed of the news, but
make each day your very own.

Beware the child who sees
his father's kindness as weakness
and his tolerance as lacking
in principles.

Youth views age with contempt,
until age views youth with
equal displeasure.

The best advice is that
which gives voice to
your own judgements.

Never assume anything 'til
you have hazarded a guess.

Sometimes first we have to find
out what something isn't, before
we can find out what it is.

In the greater scheme of
things, everything is born
and lives out its life then dies,
even the universe.

Life is like a soap bubble, it
begins with the breath of hope,
and ends with a sense of loss.

Let go the past, let it burn and in
the ashes plant a seed for today.

Success is to be found within the
orbits of combinations.

Strength is to carry the weight
of our own actions upon
our own shoulders.

Freedom is to live without fear,
yet be fearless in its defence.

Intelligence was bored so it
invented playfulness.

Mental anguish is made all
the more painful by an
inability to express it.

Better to remember our mistakes
before we repeat them.

Don't jump to conclusions until
you have carefully considered
your own footsteps.

Loneliness has hatched
many a good songbird.

Life is like a set of scales, bliss is
when both arrows meet together.

The ability to postpone reward
increases that reward ten-fold.

Learn to adapt quickly to change;
dullness leads to extinction.

Always question the impossible;
summon the improbable.

Think on your feet then
sleep on your thoughts.

Humour is that essential flux, a catalyst that welds together human differences.

In your struggles, aim to succeed; aim to inspire.

My advice to anyone searching for a goal in life is to start something inspiring, to start something new, now.

To seek in hardship is to find a flower in the desert and honey in the wilderness.

Discomfort adds a whole new
pleasure to our comforts.

Greed turns a man's heart
to stone that will slowly crush
his contentment, weigh
down all happiness.

In the midst of you all is the
treasure you seek, but is yet to be
born through the eye of a needle.

In life, we must fall on our knees,
not in prayer, but in wonder.

To those who seek a child
substitute, first find this child in
you then love and nurture it
within yourself.

To pay attention to the eyes is to
become a mind reader.

When starting a new task,
take the bull by the horns;
get going this way and you
will tame a habit.

We can learn much from animals,
like how we eat ourselves.

When worn, black is power,
absorbing all to itself, even light.

Life is a bargain, compared to the
price of eternity.

All life is close and known to us,
but we cannot remember.

We cannot heal a rotten
lifestyle; only change it.

Give yourself a holiday,
read a book.

Learn to see with your ears and
speak with your eyes.

We all have very lucky genes; we
have won the lottery of life.

Your life is etched onto your
face, like an ever-changing
landscape.

The greatest gift to your
child is your time, and
theirs to you, its absence.

Always let your curiosity
get the better of you.

When problem solving, think of
the simplest things first.

Savour life's moments; some
never leave you.

Your first struggle decides how
much more you are going to.

Distil your choices in life by
tasting each one.

Real respect must be earned;
it cannot be bought,
only grafted for.

Like a snake, we must shed
our old habits before we
can grow a new one.

To commit takes a risk, takes
enough courage to fill a sail, and
then faith in yourself to let go.

Street music puts humanity back
into the body of itself.

Impossible is when we
don't try all possibilities.

Strangely, by the action of hating
we bring that thing all the closer.

An ogre is a body without a
heart and the hero a heart but
with a conscience.

Plan according to the weather,
live according to the moment.

To fail but learn is
the key to success.

Words are but vapour
compared to deeds.

Most failures are failures
of imagination.

Always remember the power
of silence within the context
of a conversation.

Each time we lose a tooth we
gain a little wisdom.

To exercise the mind is
to think on your feet.

The secret of learning is to
be but a fellow in the turning
wheel of knowledge.

A child's innocence holds much
wisdom to test our assumptions.

Sense when something is wrong and have the good sense to speak out.

Learn to feel eggshells before you walk on them.

Your sexuality is your business, your choice, your freedom, no one else's.

Beware any insecurity that drives an interest, seeking only to accumulate to itself.

Letting go is to discover
yet another freedom.

To find ones place in the world
simply take your shoes off.

At the centre of a problem there
is usually a gut feeling.

Those who puff themselves up
to be important perhaps feel
small enough to be eaten.

Compassion takes a leap of the imagination, intelligence, humility and sensitivity, but mostly courage.

Greed is blind to itself, so indifferent to the needs of others.

Directness in speech can cut through the fog of misunderstanding and claims the ear.

Ability keeps half an eye open for improvement.

Do everything according to the
weather and you will be little
inconvenienced by it.

Give a beggar your time,
not money.

The less we have, the more we
can appreciate what we have.

Books become irrelevant when
you cannot find the right one.

Trust your instincts when there is
no time to think.

Find youth despite your age; find wisdom despite your mistakes.

Touch is like a wand, it breaks spells, makes things happen.

We pay lip service to the dead every time we eat.

Difficult as it might seem, find your vocation early, before the greater difficulty of regrets.

Aim to inspire, rather than teach.

Seek your inner compass; perhaps
you are in the right place, but
going in the wrong direction.

Stubbornness has little
to say in its defence.

Envy is a snake that bites itself.

Aim not to be liked,
but be respected.

Money earned has a power that
money given can never have.

To collect books shows a desire
to learn, but can create an
impression you've no need to.

Humour makes
light of darkness.

Gentleness is our greatest
strength; illusions of strength,
our greatest weakness.

Only words from the heart
can touch the heart.

You can always tell meanness;
it comes not from a lack of
money, but by a lack of
contentment by having it.

Stretch yourself, move your
bookshelves higher.

You can be clever as hell or be
stupid but in heavenly paradise.

People who put you in boxes,
imprison themselves.

Nothing comes from wanting everything, but anything worthwhile has often come from nothing.

Never walk in the gutter lest your aspirations and self-esteem follow.

Don't suffer fools, but help them.

Never call yourself clever instead, praise the worthiness in others.

Sensitivity and cruelty show
themselves clearly in the
line of the mouth.

Greatness is the art of giving
without thinking about it.

Paradoxically, an innocent child
can have great wisdom, for it
questions everything without
fear, seeking only the truth, so
exposing falsehoods in its quest
and zeal to learn.

Fancy a holiday in the sun?
Just pick up a book and get
tanned as you leave the
world of time behind.

Youth rebel to define themselves,
the aged become less defined.

Unhook yourself, get into the
spirit of life without alcohol; it's
a revelation, a freedom that
empowers you, not the breweries.

In the winter, prepare for
the summer; in the summer,
prepare for the winter.

Some confuse kindness with
weakness like the long lashes
of a bull's eye or a rocking
swell on a calm sea.

Necessity is the mother
of invention, playfulness
the father of discovery.

To appreciate the smallest luxury
is to savour our greatest wealth.

The desire to learn is our
greatest teacher, application our
greatest reward.

The courage to say 'no'
to another is often an
empowering 'yes' to yourself.

All life is connected, but being
transparent, we cannot see it.

Read, immerse yourself in the
imaginations of others.

A task completed
is its own reward.

With age comes that beauty of
mind called … I can't remember.

Our clothes are really costumes
for life's incredible theatre.

Regret comes through lack of
will, to speak or take a risk when
it was needed; courage is all.

Forgetting helps us
learn to remember.

Learning

No craft can be mastered
without discipline. No skill can
be mastered without time.

Learning is fun, but discovery
is life's greatest joy.

There is no glamour in death
only in what came before it.

Never be too old to acquire
learning, or too young to think
you've time to.

Experience is the best teacher; to teach is the best experience.

There would be no success without learning from failure.

Life as a human is a one-off gift from the universe; be ever grateful you are alive and strive to be a shining light in the great unfolding purpose of time.

Develop a passion for living through a love of learning.

In the sagas of history,
everything changes but people
stubbornly remain the same.

To unlock learning is to discover
its many interconnected paths
and doorways.

Loss

Often, we take people for
granted, until they die.

Sometimes when we lose
something, we gain an insight
more valuable.

At the heart of loss,
we find the gift of life.

Feeling lonely is different
to solitude; you can find
a friend in solitude.

The brave laugh through
their tears to find courage
for another day.

A thief can steal your
most valuable possession:
peace of mind.

A suicide's cry for help is often
an uncharacteristic silence.

Each day we are born, we give
birth to our dreams then die a
little death in sleep.

To make a fresh start is to clear
away the cobwebs of regret.

That we grieve for certain
material things gives a clue
as to what they replace.

Of itself, the heart cannot speak,
but when it does, you cannot.

Look back from time to time to
see how you have moved forward,
and forward just enough to serve
as a landmark to aim for.

In a sense death should be
celebrated; it gives life its urgency
and meaning.

No time is ever wasted
developing a skill.

Love and grief both have the
power to strike us dumb.

Love

To deny love to a child is to
invite evil into the world.

Let love shine like a mirror to
your friends and foes alike.

Beauty can turn to love through
the mirror of reflection.

A cat is dying to be loved,
but loves to kill.

Sex is a poor substitute
for love but it gives us
something to aim for.

It's often little details that
matter most in a relationship.

A little love makes us
strong, builds on the
foundations of security.

You may have had a loveless life
but nature has always loved you.

Respect for others
begins with yourself.

When you love what
you do, work is a joy.

Gently kindle the fires of
love; a gentle glow is better
than a singed beard.

Only real love takes good
and bad in its stride.

The unloved must find
love where they can, but don't
mistake flowers for weeds.

Bees are the sweet messengers
of symbiotic love.

Love is to own the feelings
of others, to carry their burdens
and forgive their faults.

Love is many things,
but never idleness.

Addictions are our need to
escape and avoid emotional pain.
Drugs serve our need for love,
which they cleverly mimic but
can never replace.

Forgiveness is love,
but in disguise.

A gift is to see ourselves through
the polished lens of friendship.

To find someone who believes in
you, gives you hope and
confidence to be successful;
this is love.

Respect like trust must
be earned, forgiveness
and love learned.

If you can find love in yourself, it
will touch everything you see,
every person you meet, inspire
the work you have chosen to do.

Loves empowers, but beware,
so does hate.

Love is a seed; perhaps we
shall reap what we sow.

The pain of love lost is
like a dessert without the sun,
and a forest without the sweet
song of birds.

The pain of love is
the greatest teacher.

To forgive is an act of
courage, an act of love.

There is no love without pain,
no rose without thorns.

A poem is like a flower;
its roots feed on death,
its flower speaks of love.

To love is an open
door to the moment.

To know love, one
must have lost love.

To learn to write is to slowly
fall in love with life.

Love is like the sun, it touches
all so that we can grow.

The greatest love is to be found
in the marriage of minds.

Love: the unloved are often
blind to it and the in-love
blinded by it.

An act of genuine love never dies.

To find love we must
learn to give, give it away.

Love is like a boomerang; sooner
or later it will come back to us.

Love can be found anywhere,
you must open your eyes, open
your ears, open your senses
learn to smile from your heart,
and you will find love.

Love is always in step with itself.

Work that you love has a way of
continuing onwards, staying alive.

Human love is a fine thing, but
nature's love is awesome.

To know love is to feel the
cutting edge of hope, the taste
of bliss, the storm tossed rocks
of despair.

If you can love life you can find
love, discover happiness.

The only things worth collecting
in life are love and wisdom.

To lose love is like bereavement
followed by a resurrection.

Love makes us fearless
but we must take aim.

To show your body
is to love your body.

Touch, the oldest and
first language of love.

It's no accident that the guitar
is shaped like a woman and
played by a man.

Like a tandem, to keep love
you must keep pedalling.

Love must be planted as a seed
before it can be harvested.

Love puts a spring in your step
and a smile in your heart.

In old age, the frothy head of
conversation once fermented, can
fall to a silence of understanding.

Love without touch is like winter
before the warmth of spring.

To love without possession
is to truly hold its essence.

Do not despair if love eludes
you. Be the sower of its seed,
that you may eat its fruit.

Those in the greatest need
of love should proceed with
the greatest care.

Love is a garden we must attend
to, lest it choke with weeds.

If you're not loving
you're not fully living.

To catch love one must weave
the finest web, sense the
lightest touch.

Love is to think, then act.

Lack of love delays, but cannot kill off creativity.

Love has a window, it moves, and then closes.

Let love speak through deeds, and your humanity through words that inspire deeds.

Love can be a cruel mirage; like water in the dessert, when in reality there are only sands that you are slowly sinking into.

Holding hands is the first step to love dispelling fear, showing clear intention of the symbolic bond of hearts and minds.

Gentleness and touch breaks down the strongest wall so the power of love may enter.

The language of love is gentleness, touch and communication with silence.

If you've no one to love, at least
love yourself, because love always
shines like a beacon and will
attract love to you.

Human love speaks all languages.

If there is one consolation in
our long search for love, it is
this: some beautiful stranger
is out there looking for
someone just like you.

Hope

Human generosity, when
tapped into, is like the
rain that fills an ocean.

We can move mountains;
all it takes is a shovel
and daily determination.

Forgive like the grass, love like
the sun and give like a tree.

Where there is life there is
hope, but hope without
action has no future.

We cannot hope to succeed
unless we set a target.

A freshly ploughed field
is an ocean to a seagull.

An enquiring mind
will feed itself.

Through the struggle of
self-knowledge we
slowly move forward.

A song is a poem with wings.

Many more things bind
humanity than divide it.

When people work for a
common good they can move
mountains of cynicism and
drain swamps of apathy.

Our doubts are our fears;
mere shadows compared
to the light of courage.

If you lack a friend, take
up the pen, you will
find one straightaway.

To laugh at our fears
is to conquer them.

There is enough sorrow in
the world to fill an ocean; only
a rainbow makes light of it.

A friend points out your faults
instead of telling others.

In solitude we find a
friend in ourselves.

Arm yourself against despair
by seeing the absurd and
funny things in life.

Each person has a spirit guide
within themselves.

Those who persist will develop,
whatever their talent or ability.

Harmony needs more than one
string to make it happen.

A bird is a gift made perfect by
time flying high on the wings of
the impossible.

A poem is a flower with
roots in the heart.

The gulf between nations,
can it be bridged with love,
like a rainbow?

The world is full of friendly,
hospitable loving, fantastic,
inspiring and adorable people,
don't let any newspaper or
cynical TV programme
tell you differently.

See depression as a
cloud that hides the sun.

A smile breaks down
human barriers, like the
sun through the clouds.

In every sense, old age is
our second childhood.

We are never alone; our ancestors
are always with us, urging us on.

There is no belief more
life changing than believing
in yourself.

Hope can weave a web of
falsehoods; better a small
certainty to build on.

Confidence is like a small
child; nurture it well.

When we meditate, we
clean the lens of our soul.

Music is the soul of man
and a prayer to life.

Achievement is
repeatable, I repeat.

The best solution is
often the simplest one.

Try to see the
opportunity in change.

Living positively is to love
and embrace challenge.

We stretch ourselves when
we have to then discover the
strength of trying.

Each new day is a gift,
a fresh start, another
opportunity, to get it right.

With disabilities often comes the
gift of other special abilities.

If you are good at one thing, you
can succeed in others.

Success in one is the door
that opens many.

When seeking a miracle,
remember that you are one.

Sometimes the toughest
moments in life are ones that
help us the most.

To keep a diary is to turn the
pages of your own later recovery.

The pure innocence of a child
is like a twinkling star; its
light shines through the
darkness of all humanity.

When we push hard at
difficulties, we push open a
hidden door of possibilities.

Be a sparkle of light in
a stream of consciousness.

A smiling face can lodge itself
in your memory to inspire
you when you cannot.

A handle on a problem is to
halve the problem.

Often, when things are starting
to go wrong they are beginning
to turn out right.

While you can, always ride on
the top deck of the bus.

Take heart, from a glimpse of
your own, from a stranger.

To find hope we must learn to
love and believe in humanity.

Learning is an open door
to a life worth living.

If you have started upon
a journey continue; do not
stop until you have reached
your destination.

Kindness has a ripple effect,
moving outwards, touching
the lives of others, like the
sunlight on water.

Confidence is like the bow wave
of a ship; met head on it can cut
through many storms.

To do the impossible,
begin with the possible.

Each day without fail, do one
thing you love to do.

There is an answer to every
problem if we seek it from every
direction and every angle.

If you have a voice,
a conscience and a pen,
you can change the world.

Learn to make things happen by
arriving at the destination you
thought you'd never see.

Try to dance through life; each
step turns pain into pleasure.

To keep going, hold the words
in a song, a poem in a smile.

The pen is mightier than
the sword because it can heal
wounds, forgive enemies
and convey love.

Don't condemn a whole tree for
just one bad apple; learn to
savour all that is good.

If you have no land, cultivate
your mind; if you have no
castle, strengthen your body;
if you have no family, open
your heart to a stranger.

Human love speaks all languages.

We can do almost the impossible
when prepared for all
possibilities.

Friends and family

If you give a child all it wants, it will never fight for what it needs.

A friend is only as good as the friends they keep.

Youth rebels to define itself and its time.

Observe how difficulties test loyalties and friendships.

To remember an old forgotten
tune is like a visit from
a dear friend.

Be a good gardener to your
friend's estate; they cannot always
tell flowers from weeds.

Learn to enjoy the company
of others so as to savour
time on your own.

The family is a sacred
cow, but with horns.

Your family expects loyalty and respect but can be your harshest critic; giving no quarter, showing no mercy in its judgments.

Truth is a gift amongst friends; a boil lanced will heal quickly.

You cannot buy friendship but money can certainly ruin it.

To be inspired is to learn by the example of others.

Every friend is a teacher, but we must listen.

A simple word or two to a
stranger can be an intervention
against loneliness.

Talk to everyone; reach out,
touch your human family.

To choose your friends is to steer
your own destiny.

Shared hardships bind
souls forever.

To struggle makes you stronger,
but is less needed when you have
good friends around you.

To live, share our lives
with others, teaches us
about ourselves.

Cleanse your heart so that you
can be a true mirror to your
friend's soul.

In friendship, seek an open
face, a firm hand, and
a generous heart.

Often in the midst of despair is
found the very flower of
humanity, and in the roots of
sister and brotherhood, we
discover ourselves.

Gather up your own thoughts;
also question the thoughts
of others.

Giving is Nature's finest
example for living.

A friend in need, is the friend
you have yet to call.

Empathy is to walk in other peoples' shoes.

Find a passion large or small, and you will find a friend.

Friendship dispels the myth of separateness.

Sometimes it costs just a fiver to find out who our friends are.

Seek a marriage of minds upon the road of understanding.

Beauty is nothing compared to
the fusion of two minds.

Make your best
friend your mind.

Friendships that are built
on hardships have been tested
by time and, if not broken,
become stronger.

Test a friend like
you'd test a rope.

Finding friends is like mining;
if you're lucky you will
find a diamond.

Your friends are your fortune, or
ill fortune, on the road to life.

Beware new friends that come
in-between and change
established friendships.

Insults and laughter move
a friendship forward;
miscommunication and
money, backwards.

Judge a person by what they do,
compared to what they say.

To learn to carry the burdens of
others is to see your own.

By sharing what we have,
we yield a human harvest.

Your friends are your teacher's
pupils, and your pupils, your
teacher's friends.

Sharing underpins the
very foundations of
friendship and love.

Companionship brings
peace to cows and pasture.

A sound friendship takes
note of silence and silence
lets friendship speak.

Feelings of loneliness are
often a reaction to change;
from having been with people
to the adjustment of being
on your own again.

The greatest friends are the ones
who inspire you and, in some
strange way, never leave you.

The qualities I admire most
in people are generosity
then humour.

If you can, keep money out of
friendship, for money curses
everything it touches.

Encouragement is a powerful
incentive to try harder, and when
we do will always surprise us.

Nature and philosophy

To sing is to enter
into peoples' hearts.

Nature is my church,
my conscience a candle
floating on water.

Mankind cannot destroy
nature, only himself.

Equilibrium unfolds the
universe; there is a point of
balance in all things.

We can learn a lot from trees;
they don't move around, but put
down roots, and bear fine fruit.

How great is the human
mind, but also how wicked
in its perversity.

The dexterity of the human hand
is absolutely amazing, a million
years of evolution most of us
simply take for granted.

A good portrait painter is half
artist half geologist.

We are what we eat and
become what we think.

Nature inspires, gives solace,
heals the spirit, always forgiving.

Music is the science of
harmony, a key that unlocks
the soul of the cosmos.

Each person is a cell in
the body of humanity.

To start a spiritual life,
first prepare a garden.

The bee has made the blossom
and the blossom made the bee,
thus is paradise made.

Through human laughter,
strangely, dolphins recognise
themselves.

Food for thought is a walk
through trees where often a
branch in the mind awaits
bearing fruit.

A tree's strength comes from
layers of growth; age has the
same effect.

To understand landscape
you have to walk it.

Two great muses that will
always make me stand in awe:
the moon reflected in water.

Nature gives us innocent clues to
the origins of existence, like
dappled sunny day clouds on the
back of a pony, or the barred
feathers of a falcon's wing.

External beauty only hints
at our internal perfection.

Motherhood is the bedrock
of all possible futures.

To grow something from
a seed is to plant another.

An avenue of trees paved
the way, they still do.

We each have two drums,
strings in tension and a set of
bagpipes to blow on.

Strangely, it's natures built in
imperfection that makes
everything work so perfectly.

What gift, the tree, a living
metaphor for life itself.

Never kill a fly for another;
it kills twice.

Respect and honour nature's
laws, fear and question all others.

When you wish to turn over a
new leaf tell the branches that
made you, the roots of the tree,
the soil that sustains you.

We pass through life and all life passes through us, only water remains unchanged.

When you dance, imagine you are turning like a galaxy and in perfect step with that great mystery and symphony of the universe, for we are one.

Respect all birds; they invented flight 300 million years before we did.

We are what we eat, but seldom think what we plant.

Sometimes we need a silent
retreat, where we can find our
centre, let healing begin its work,
content just to be, to write, to
think, to walk with, knowing we
are part of nature, in this way we
are never alone in solitude.

First comes the wind then
the rain; to read the weather
is to save a storm.

To be still with nature,
is to fill with nature.

To paint or draw the human
body is to glimpse its time-honed
beauty and perfection.

Sex is to bare all
for future relations.

Faith, religion and belief

The ultimate blasphemy is to kill
another in the name of religion.

The best form of evangelism
is to be happy.

Youth always brings a fresh
dynamic into the world; we
must have faith in their visions,
their humanity.

Real strength comes from
admitting our weakness,
knowing our faults.

The worst things can bring the
best qualities out in us.

A person must be a good servant
to their conscience.

In matters of faith we cannot
all wear the same shoes,
but some try.

Make your kitchen an altar,
your table a thanksgiving.

Religion runs in straight lines,
but the spirit is a perfect circle.

When you have nothing you
have to build it stone by stone,
so too is trust.

To act is to have
the courage to fail.

The problem with God, he
gives power to religion.

Religion is power,
but someone else's.

To err is human; to have
the courage to forgive is
next to godliness.

To some extent all religion is
based on fear, the fear of death.

Respect the beliefs of others,
mould and change your own
(avoid religion).

It is better to believe than
not, a man who believes
nothing has yet to live.

No plant can grow without
roots, so is belief.

Dynastic corruption is always
ascension at the highest levels.

Evangelists are like drowning
men, they clutch at others
to save themselves.

The Church admonishes sins, but
tells the biggest lies.

The first law of godliness is
compassion; the second is
action upon the first.

The church is a
monopoly of souls.

Religion is a cage for birds.
Fear puts them there.

Another's faith is like a boat,
do not rock it but be the
wind that fills its sails.

Man made God in his own
image, not the other way round.

The symbolism of the tie is
wasted on a priest, for they carry
the white badge of exemption.

A gardener is probably closer
to the roots of an after-life
than any minister.

When people talk of paradise
in the next world, I tell
them to open their eyes.

Experience at the lowest
levels will prepare us
for the higher ones.

Better to act than pray, better to
speak out than remain silent.

There is much to be said for the hidden riches of an aesthetic life.

The strange thing about karma is people often become the very thing they hate the most.

Our destiny will gently nudge us through our feelings until we take decisive action.

We have all arrived in heaven as angels, only to create merry hell.

Fate and fortune

The doors of opportunity are
opening and closing all the time,
one simply has to be alert
enough and brave enough to walk
through them.

Like a play, life is short;
fill it with adventure and
fine drama, aim for an
encore and a good end.

Let habit be your slave,
not your master.

Meanness is like a desert in
the heart, nothing grows
there except thorns.

Luck is like the wind, only
a good sailor can master
it to their advantage.

To understand our own patterns
of behaviour is to put a handle
on our own destiny.

Enlightenment is to see our
own lives mirrored in the
writings of another.

To adventure out on a peril-less
voyage is to discover ourselves.

Courage to be yourself
is the finest chivalry.

The best luck in the world is that
which we can make ourselves.

Don't make the nails for your
own bed of nails.

Suffering is a hard teacher,
but it can bring the gift
of enlightenment.

Hell is the inferno
of incurable disease.

To waste your time is foolish;
to waste your life is regrettable
but to waste talent is a crime
against life itself.

Injustice ploughs a deep
furrow, in the brow.

A face is like a changing
landscape; every ridge
and furrow a story.

A few timely words can change
outcomes for a lifetime.

Intelligence is reflected in the
eyes, spirituality in the feet.

Do not pass through life silently.

We all have three wise men
to guide us: intuition,
judgement, and reason.

Take care when we accuse
others lest we impale ourselves
on our own sword.

Do not make a meal of
regret, 'tis to chew on
our own excrement.

Melancholy is a dark cloud
that can sometimes hide
a bright light.

To those that swear, let them
chew on their own words.

You cannot go wrong if you
do the right things for
the right reasons.

To be intelligent and to have a sharp wit is a fine thing but take care how you swing the blade, lest you cut off your own head.

Alcohol lights the flame of romance but pisses on the roses.

There is danger in darkness, only ignorance is darker.

Heaven and hell do exist, but only here on Earth.

The downtrodden seek power; the victim seeks revenge.

Insecurity is not an illness,
but a trauma that spreads out
through one's entire life,
wrecking everything.

Life has given us a dawn and
dusk for all our endeavours.

Sensitivity is both a
blessing and a curse.

Alcohol is the hemlock of love.

Of people, speak only well, for
bad deeds broadcast themselves.

Who gives of themselves
will find themselves.

Tragedy is always the
timely combination
of deadly circumstances.

When we knock on the
door of need, we stir the
abundance of the universe.

Theatre is a looking glass, a
spotlight on the stage of
our own destiny.

Choice is the master sailor at the helm of our own destiny.

To become cynical in old age is to have one foot in the grave.

Take care where you place your ladder in life, as one rung tends to lead to another.

Your fate can turn on a sixpence, if you have one.

To be aware of your own neediness is to reset the balance of your fortunes.

Like the atom, we are all bound
to one another upon the
deck of a greater one.

Half of success is being in the
wrong place at the right time.

Often a journey of struggle
is a voyage of discovery.

Suicide is not the end of your
troubles, but the very beginning.

Most people have an angel
on one shoulder and the devil
on the other.

To leave things to fate
is to invite misfortune.

Look at how something might
end before you begin it.

As we age we become closer to
our childlike selves, slowly
walking backwards towards the
door we came through.

The songs that you take to your
heart will save your soul.

To attract the most beautiful moth we must burn with the brightest light.

Aye, have pity for the living dead, but not the dead, for they live under our feet.

Life is but a dream that we must wake from, lest we die.

Somehow, the greater the intelligence, the greater the capacity for evil when the balance of the mind tips the other way.

Everyone has an inheritance;
the accrued genius and wisdom
of our forefathers, and to all
distant ancestors it is given
freely as a gift.

Good fortune is like a ball that
we must learn to catch.

Those who look, but can see,
those who listen and can hear,
those who dream but can do, to
these few, are riches given.

One loose spoke can weaken
the wheel of progress.

Future

Man is born of creativity, but
we must find the keys to unlock
it within ourselves.

The future is in the hands of
good teachers to small children.

A good teacher can only point
the way to learning.

Only when we truly know
ourselves can we fix our compass
and steer a true course.

We can do almost the
impossible when prepared
for all possibilities.

What is intelligence
without a soul?

To define art is to
define humanity.

We must be ruthless in
our search for knowledge,
compassionate in
how we apply it.

Do something no one else
has done, see something no
one else has seen, think
the unthinkable dream.

Intent is the pre-selection gear
that gets things moving.

Intelligence can work for good
or evil, has the power to build
or destroy. Thankfully, it
gives us the choice.

The artist should always
be modest about their own
work, seek to learn.

It's doubtful if computers will ever match the minds of human beings, they will always live in the shadow of our imagination.

Learn from nature who only takes what she needs, but gives in abundance.

Unwittingly, man constructs complex infrastructure to mirror our bodies.

Compassion in society is always a gauge of its humanity and tolerance.

We only have so much time,
think of thread coming off the
end of a bobbin reel.

That access to education helps
people with mental ill health is
clear; that it helps society at large
has yet to be discovered.

Science, the arts, music,
literature, philosophy; are they
not all fellows joined at the hub
in the great wheel of knowledge.

Humanity is a child in the
universe of mind.

To make peace, we must walk
and talk with our enemies.

We inherit the world from our
ancestors but not the future.

In the midst of mankind lies an
undiscovered kingdom.

To change the world start
something, make something.

Befriending the vulnerable
defends all our futures.

Real modern-day heroes are
those who cycle and shun the car.

Consider how you would survive
in a desert, much of humanity
has made the earth so.

Death is like a deep sleep, but
without the dreams.

The future is just an idea, a
vision yet to be born.

When we try to remove all
risk from life, we remove
all life from existence.

Begin a project as soon as
it presents itself. Start well
with a good push; imagine a
flywheel turning, this inertia
will carry you forward over
most difficulties.

Every brick, a life laid down,
every stone step a discovery. For
in life we are not alone, the past
lives on with audacity.

Humans have God-like powers,
but with ape-like mood swings.

War and peace

False ideas sown can grow
weeds of religious hate.

Resentment is that lull
before the kettle boils.

Learn to read between the
lines before the writing
on the wall appears.

Terrorism seems to have
the opposite effect of that
intended; it strengthens
our spirit and resolve.

Violence and war never
achieved anything but more
violence and war.

The root of war is fear;
the root of peace is trust.

Warmongers are buyers of
souls and sellers of coffins.

War is the last resort of power
and greed; we are the pawns.

The only just war is against
poverty, disease and ignorance.

If we can prevent war, we have
won a greater battle.

Those who triumph in
violence, take humanity
back to the dinosaurs.

Fear is a terrible weapon in the
armoury of our imagination.

War seems to be the midwife
of change: social and
technological. In this way
mankind staggers forward
until the next breech birth.

Shame we cannot unpick our
long evolved ancestral biology
and swap violence for
competitive sports.

Peace is a seed sown in the
minds of children; a poppy
in the field of war.

Where there is no bridge
for peace, go build the
foundations for one.

A uniform gives the wearer
status, power and identity, but
there are strings attached.

The shadow of disease and
pestilence follow all wars,
a ghostly reminder of the
real enemy that we should
all be fighting.

Love and war inspire
the greatest poets.

The element of surprise works
in both love and war.

To be anti-war is to be pro-life.

Making war on our smallest
enemies will bring the largest
benefit to all humanity.

War is never worth one life,
but it can take just one life
to prevent it.

Exchanging fruit in a conflict,
not missiles, will plant an
orchard for peace everlasting.

The pen is mightier than the
sword, but is also the healer
of wounds.

Money and power

Let poverty speak to our
humanity and teach us humility.

Greed is like a plague of
locusts; it fattens itself
whilst others starve.

Stature is greater than power;
generosity greater than money.

Life has many poverties,
meanness of spirit is one of the
greatest wildernesses.

Despite hardship, the school of
poverty teaches us generosity.

Money can make men mean
and blind to the real
wealth of contentment.

Wealth is an illusion.
The wealthy are often
poor and unhappy; tis a
great thing to be free of
want, but still be able to give.

Austerity focuses the mind,
furnishes the imagination, gives
survival its edge.

No man is poor if he
plays an instrument,
can draw, or write poetry.

The problem with money given,
it doesn't carry the same weight
as money earned.

Money would be friendless,
without greed.

Money corrupts everything
it touches, fills all voids
except the grave.

Let money go to the devil,
but keep your wit.

If money is blood, then landlords
and lenders are vampires.

Real wealth is talent, and worthy
of respect always.

Never mix business dealings with
alcohol or you'll have more than
a hangover to worry about.

I sometimes wonder how much
we own our possessions, and in
reality how much they own us.

Materialism is a distraction;
at its worst, a poor substitute
for happiness.

It's strange how selfishness
and greed are never satisfied.

Those who love money
will never find the happiness
of contentment.

Strange, how such little money
blinds those who kill and
slaughter our wild, priceless
and irreplaceable animals.

To wonder and appreciate is the greater way to own anything.

If money is power, think whom you are giving it to.

If there must be a devil, surely this must be money and all who worship it, rob others for it and kill in its name.

The antidote to the curse of money is to start to give it away, and in this way, discover wealth and happiness.

To live modestly within
your means is the wealth that
will save you from poverty
and the burden of excess.

To endure poverty is to
receive the best education
that money cannot buy.

There is a wealth more valuable
than money that builds
communities, more resilient than
any economy, even war cannot
destroy it.

Crime and punishment

Gangs often represent a
crisis of identity, split
loyalties and insecurities.

The seed of violence is in
every human being, but the
seed of love can only be
planted by another.

The adder quickly strikes
out against its enemies, so
must we against falsehood.

In truth, the crafty and cunning
often make snares for themselves.

Beware the human predator; they
can sense weakness in others.

A suspicious mind generally
hides an ignorant one.

There is no evil, only
ignorance and sickness.

A criminal has a keen
sense of justice and revenge.

When one person turns to
crime, all humanity suffers.

The feelings of powerlessness,
isolation and alienation can
be an explosive mix.

Perhaps violence against women
is jealousy for a greater power
that men can never possess.

Health

We own our bodies,
but must answer to the
greater body of humanity.

Clutter is an overcrowded
room in the mind.

Things can obscure a greater
thing in ourselves.

Lack of self-esteem can create a
void that others fill.

Empathy is born of suffering,
patience from understanding.

Our health is all we have;
a visit to the hospital puts
all in perspective.

Measure a long life by the
yardstick of one wholesome day.

Good health is often
down to good habits.

To find youth in old age, one
must have courage, enthusiasm
and a little daring.

If you feel you are in the wrong place, remember your heart is always in the right place.

Eat little, but savour each morsel like a banquet.

Only hunger can satisfy, fatigue brings sound sleep.

Respect begins with your own body.

People strive for diamonds, but a drop of water is far more precious.

Beware! Alcohol opens
doors, then the cages of wild
animals, then trap doors
down to a snake pit.

To take a walk is to give our
mind a much-needed holiday.

Learn to look after yourself;
you may have a big heart,
but only the one.

Reading can do for the
mind what exercise can do
for the body.

Don't hug the bruises but
celebrate the healing.

Listen to your heart for
guidance but also follow its
incredible example.

Drink when you thirst
for knowledge; eat when you
hunger for truth.

Treat your body like a God
so it can work miracles.

Neurosis is a painful
shadow of a real event.

Worry will help shorten your life; good food, exercise, hope and a purpose extend it.

Happiness

A smile has the power to
disperse clouds, like the sun.

The secret of happiness is to
love what you do, and do
what you love to do.

Learning is our greatest joy
always to be rediscovered.

When we have less, we grow
more in happiness.

The companion to
contentment is laughter.

Happiness is a flower in bloom.

Self-knowledge gives us courage
to root out fear.

Fear is the enemy of
opportunity and happiness.

Sometimes you have to
begin to start, before you
can start to begin.

Happiness is to also discover
what makes other people happy.

The greatest belief is self-belief
but we need others to gift it.

Do a little of what you need to,
a little of what you love to do,
every day and you will be
happy, and tomorrow will
take care of itself.

Joy is when your heart is in
your work but a pain held
in the heart, breaks it.

To watch the sun rise and
set each day is a simple
but profound joy.

For inspiration look outward,
for guidance look inward.

Happiness is made all
the greater by sharing it.

See health as wealth,
contentment as happiness.

Depression is to live in the
shadow of your happiness.

Children can take us back to that
magic place which we have all
travelled through.

The secret of happiness
is to replace material wealth
for spiritual riches.

A happy child at play cleanses
all the worlds' moans.

Aim for the greater happiness of
contentment through the
fulfilment of your aspirations.

Many a spoke has stopped the
wheel of happiness turning.

When you dance, the universe
dances with you.

To gain possession of yourself
you have to fight for what
you believe in.

Be on constant guard against
clutter, an archenemy of clarity
and contentment.

Always aim to have fun;
happiness depends on it.

When there is no happiness,
there are only symbols of
happiness to play with.

Unhappy are those who ever
want more, for greed can never
be satisfied; only giving brings
abundance and contentment.

To live well is to choose
well; choices are infinite,
so too is happiness.

All nature exists in a balanced equilibrium and we must somehow find that point within ourselves, for here sits the happiness of contentment.

Learn to read your dreams, until they cease to be.

To find the root cause of our desires is to gently unburden our need of them, gain knowledge of ourselves and lasting happiness.

Doing what you love will
release you to love the things
you don't enjoy.

To be grateful plants
the seed of contentment.

Being alone without certainty is
often where we discover that rock
beneath our feet.

Look someone square in the
eye when you wish to say NO,
then they get it.

There is risk in everything,
especially when we do nothing.

Happiness is something
we must find for ourselves
then share with others.

Don't confuse the success of
others with your own success.

Think of writing as your
soul companion, in truth the
opposite of loneliness.

Cast out the many things
that obstruct us and distract
us from life's simple aims.

Take the weight of the world
off your shoulders and discover
the giant in yourself.

Truth

Arrogance is ignorance on stilts.

Seekers after truth learn from the
school of silence.

Sometimes silence can act as a
mirror for bad speech.

Envy tells you how bad
someone thinks they are.

To be human is surely to
rise above mere existence.

A little white lie can cast
a long shadow of doubt.

The strange thing about
secrets is we have to tell
everyone about them.

Belief is a most powerful and
potent force for action, for good
things, equally for destruction.

Let your guts feel the way with
matters of the heart.

In truth wisdom is born
of nakedness.

Speak out, lest silence
be our own accuser.

A complement from the
heart is worth more than
a room full of speeches.

Intelligence shows itself in the
eyes, cruelty in the mouth.

No man is wise who
has yet not fallen.

Art and science have things
in common, they share the
same root: observation.

When children speak they
sometimes show us all the
barriers to honesty.

Information is power,
but not wisdom.

Without language there is no
thought. Think about it.

Treat an ignorant man like a
dangerous animal.

Nothing was ever achieved
without effort, no obstacle
overcome without determination.

Hats have a clever way of telling
others what's on their minds.

Gentleness is strength,
but in disguise.

Everything changes in history
except human nature.

The root of anger
is often powerlessness.

Power over others often produces
its own blindness.

Alcohol sometimes removes the
masks of those who hide.

Humiliation is a
wound that never heals.

People can justify anything
if the lies are big enough.

Revenge only adds
one wrong to another.

Separateness is an
illusion, for all is one.

189

EUREKA! Discovery
is our greatest joy!

Truth gives you a sword for your
courage and a light to sweep
away your enemies.

To expect is to
hasten the probability.

I love the eye because through
the eye of a person I can
see two souls.

We can sense when something
is wrong even though
the truth eludes us.

Be true to yourself, life is too
short to be anyone else.

To complete anything well is to
place you on a springboard for
your next endeavour.

The wise listen before they
speak and chew words well
before they swallow.

Follow your heart,
but not over a cliff.

Envy talent but never money.

Wisdom is the art of
speaking without talking.

Wisdom is to assume less
and question more.

Truth is a sharp sword, piercing
both heart and tongue.

Honesty is like a light,
cutting through the fog
of mixed messages.

We've put our heads in the
sand for thirty years, to destroy
the last thirty thousand.

Your conscience is the highest
authority you must answer to,
it stands above all others,
including God.

If you can engage your brain,
then to lose is to win.

Some people live
only words apart.

In truth, laughter echoes our
fears and personal pain.

Some people like to knock
your confidence because
they don't have any.

To journey down the deepest
mine shaft is to know the light.

In truth, to draw on life is to
draw upon the waters of eternity.

Creativity

Creativity is like a cistern that
slowly fills itself after every flush.

To write we need to
feel connected even in
our own separateness.

Through writing we can
share our deepest thoughts,
describe our experiences, inspire
others to imagine the impossible,
confirm our existence and
common humanity.

Ideas are like blending tea, there
is always room for improvement.

Our hands are the foot
soldiers for all our endeavours,
faithful messengers of the
mind's many imaginings.

If you can sign your name
you can draw. If you can draw,
you can write poetry.

Learn to use what you have
around you; your creative mind
will soon astound you.

Don't wait around for
inspiration. We have to start
doing before the muses appear.

Writing a poem is like cooking,
always use fresh ingredients.

The poet's lot is pain
and suffering isolation
but not poverty.

Grubs emerge from their
cocoons, miraculously
transformed, like poets.

Think of a lion in a cage
which must be contained
or it will kill its keeper. My
pen writes between the bars.

Writing is like knitting, first you
put some lines down, and then it
slowly begins to take shape.

Writing helps you know
yourself, to notice the world
around you, and express yourself
with clarity; where did we go
wrong teaching it?

Writing can be like a mirror; see
yourself in a new light.

Art is our celebration of being
human; the flower of
consciousness is aesthetics.

Man is born of
creativity, I repeat.

A diamond has many sides;
so does creativity.

Our imagination
is THE greatest artist.

To be creative is to paint
yourself into a fine landscape.

The muses need a sacrifice before
they will give of themselves.

Writing is to become aware
of other unexplored dimensions;
you go wide across uninhabitable
plains, deep into your darkest
thoughts, into subterranean
vaults of the subconscious
mind, or fly high on the
wings of your imagination.

Within the lifecycle of a butterfly
lies the secret of creativity.

Creativity transcends all
attempts at its captivity.

I do defer to a greater artist who
paints the skies, and cries in
anger at our blindness.

To be creative is to step
into another world only
then to find yourself.

Creativity is a step on the
road to recovery, discovery,
integration and belonging.

To find ourselves is
to discover a universe.

The genius of art is that very
thing with which the artist
struggles to express.

Art is the catalyst, the
unrecognised maker of humanity.

Catch something beautiful
or poignant and bring it
to life through art.

Words can feel inadequate when
expressing emotions; this is
where art and music excel.

Creativity is the only marriage
without a partner.

Creativity is as much about
destruction as construction.

Often, the longer you spend on a
drawing the more you will
struggle with it.

Your painting is half your model,
half yourself.

In our self-portrait, we must
embrace all our perfections and
imperfections.

The history of writing is
like a tree, a poet being a bird
singing in its branches.

The goal of an artist or
musician should be to inspire
rather than entertain.

To sing the songs of
others is often prostitution
to a songwriter.

Make creativity your faithful
and constant friend.

Draw with words, and imagine a
landscape that others shall walk.

In art as in music, one has
to risk one's own skin.

See creativity not as leisure
but as work, our great gift to
change the world.

Discipline gives creativity a
framework to build on, a space
where playfulness and freedom
can play from, a well that other
artists can draw on.

Good art is good when it can
speak to all generations.

If you are creative, commit yourself to it; this is a marriage that will help you find happiness and fulfilment.

The hand has a voice, like the mind has a presence.

To grow something, is to plant yourself.

The most important job of a writer is to be able to hit the waste paper basket at ten feet.

Writing helps us to harvest
our thoughts, so we can
endure a famine.

The pen is the key that
opens a thousand doors.

When I think, a miracle returns.

Music

Music is an open
door to the moment.

Music is eternity,
speaking to humanity.

To dance is to express the
spiritual embodiment of our
human existence, a celebration of
joy in life's perfection.

At its best, music can describe
time; express eons of it.

To hate a song is to remember it.

In the beginning was music;
the Bang came later.

If music conveys one thing,
it's the complexity and beauty
of our universe.

Music is, in essence,
beautiful mathematics.

Music is the soul of the universe
visiting the mind of another.

A band is a family tied together
with the strings and chords of
musical emotions.

Let a song enter your ears that
will befriend your heart.

Politics and society

The task of democracy is to deny power to those who would take it from us and take us back to the dark ages.

Beware the newspaper that tells you what to think, the flickering box that turns off your brain.

Like a cuckoo, once in the nest a politician sets about to destroy the competition.

History tends to repeat itself, but
then so do all politicians.

Avoid the news or reading
the papers, this will only
depress you. Instead, throw out
the TV and begin making,
creating your own news.

Power that decorates itself
must be wallpaper.

It's always an achievement if you
generate some opposition in
what you are trying to achieve.

Let injustice make you angry,
make you act, make you strong.

Challenge absurdities
with laughter.

Putting people first before
profit ensures any investment
will grow and multiply.

Hypocrisy is to ban smoking
on the grounds of health, but
meanwhile allow traffic pollution
to kill off the entire nation.

Our one vote should always
be a reminder of how just one
idiot in power can be the
grief of millions.

Those who rob us have no
integrity with which to govern.

Never think you are so great that
you cannot improve, or
undermine your achievements by
singing your own praises.

Slaves build the greatest
monuments to their masters.

A politician promises the earth
but crows from a dunghill.

A politician tries to talk from his
heart but the motion is passed at
the other end.

Put the art of listening before
the art of speaking.

Even potatoes have eyes, corn
have ears, and yet people ignore
world hunger.

My Thanks

To Nick Rowe for his kind offer to publish this book. To Hilary Bailey and all of the Converge staff who've encouraged me along the way. To Lesley Jenyns who patiently typed up all my original manuscripts. To Kathleen Renwick who helped me during the editing and book assembly process. To Alex Weston for her professional help and caring guidance. To Tom Nightingale who introduced me to Converge. And finally, to Converge which has done so much to help me turn my life around. My biggest thanks must go to them.